100 Animals
Adult Coloring
Book

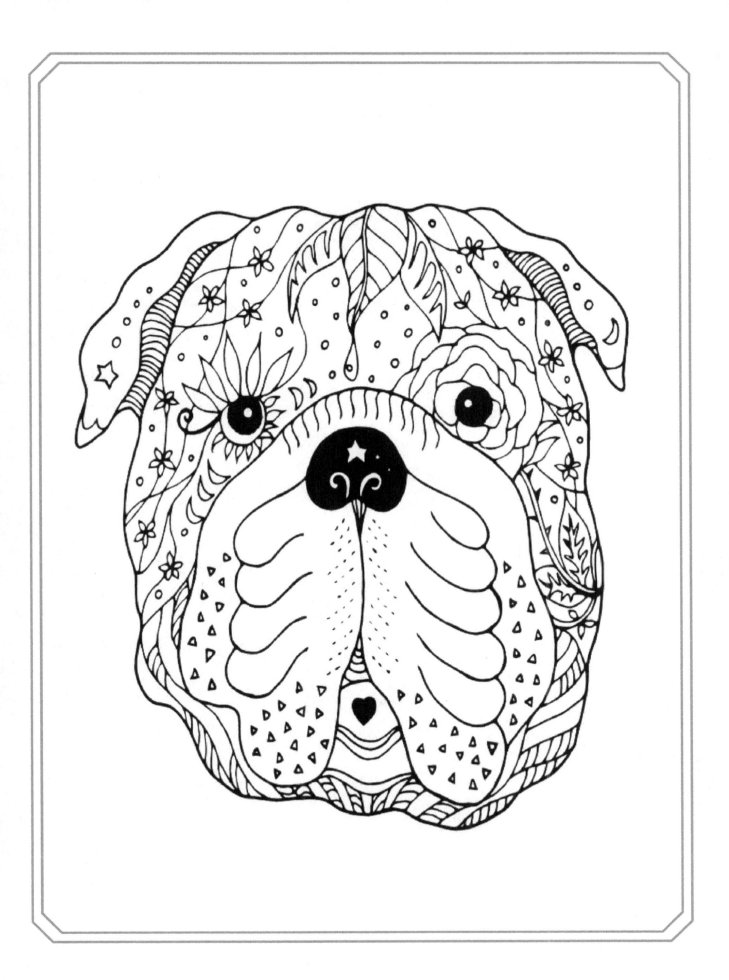

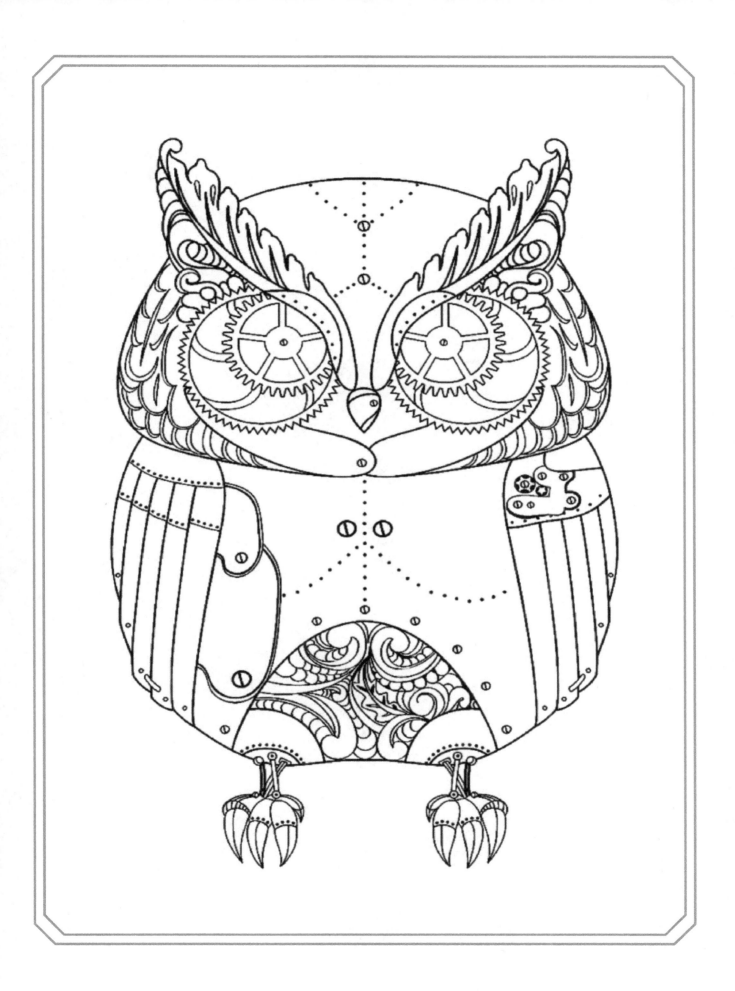

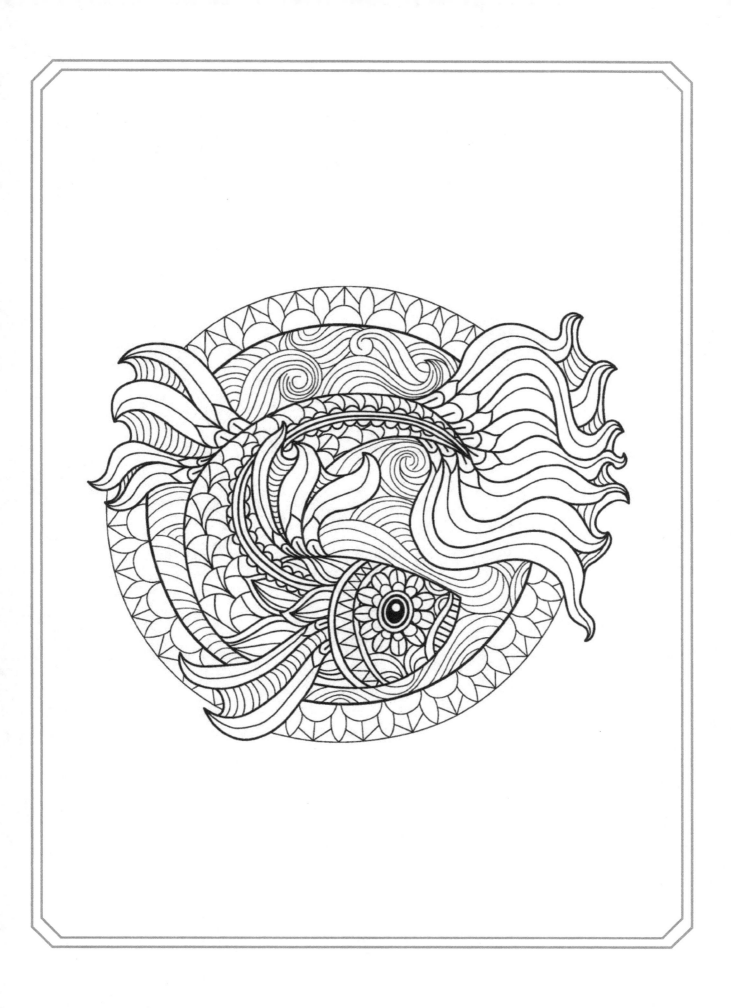

Thank you!

We hope you enjoyed our book.

As a small family company, your feedback is very important to us.

Please let us know how you like our book at:

infobooks.creators@gmail.com

CPSIA information can be obtained
at www.ICGtesting.com
Printed in the USA
LVHW061605210621
690766LV00003B/454